Fun Collec[...]

from the 1950s[...]

A Handbook & Price Guide

an Lindenberger

with Dana Cain

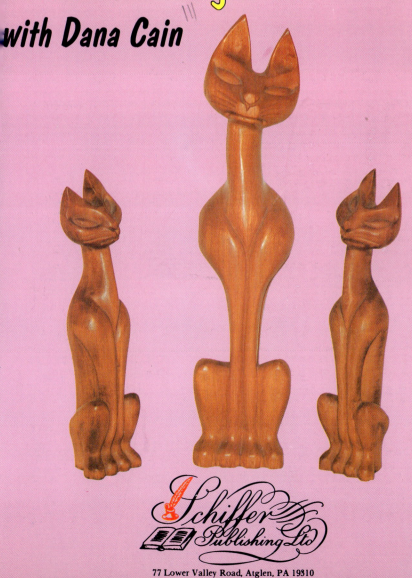

Schiffer Publishing Ltd

77 Lower Valley Road, Atglen, PA 19310

Printed in China

ISBN: 0-88740-888-5

Book Design by Audrey L. Whiteside

Library of Congress Cataloging-in-Publication Data

Lindenberger, Jan.
    Fun collectibles from the 1950s, 60s, & 70s/Jan Lindenberger with Dana Cain.
        p.   cm.
    ISBN 0-88740-888-5 (softcover)
    1. Popular culture--Collectibles--United States--Catalogs.
    I. Cain, Dana.   II. Title.
NK808.L55   1996
973.92'075--dc20   95-37091
                                                      CIP

Published by Schiffer Publishing Ltd.
77 Lower Valley Road
Atglen, PA 19310
Please write for a free catalog.
This book may be purchased from the publisher.
Please include $2.95 for shipping.
Try your bookstore first.

We are interested in hearing from authors with book ideas on related subjects.

CONTENTS

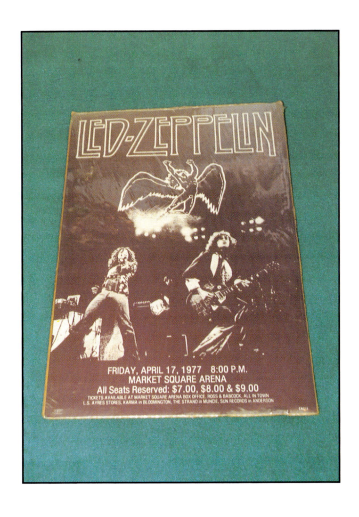

Acknowledgments

A very special thank you to Dana Cain from Atomic Antiques and Collectibles in Denver. She opened up her home and allowed me to photograph her wonderful and extensive collection. Also for giving me most of the information for this book.

Also thanks to:

Harriet White, Brighton, Colorado

Antique Gallery, Colorado Springs, Colorado

Flamingo Road, Denver, Colorado

Colorado Antique Gallery, Littleton, Colorado

Collectors Corner, Northglen, Colorado

Lisa's Antique Mall , Divernon, Illinois

Moonlite Gardens Mall. Litchfield, Illinois

Illinois Antique center, Peoria, Illinois

Lucky Lindy's art deco-thru 50's-60's, Peoria, Illinois

Mike and Donna Miller, East Peoria, Illinois

Springfield Antique Mall, Springfield, Illinois

South County Antique Mall, St. Louis, Missouri

Apple Wagon Antique Mall, Williamsburg, Missouri

INTRODUCTION

Unlike generations before us, we who grew up in the 50s, 60s and 70s share more common memories, thanks to television. We played with the same toys, thanks to TV commercials. We had the same teen idols, we wore the same groovy clothes. We all drank Funny Face. We all had a Slinky. We all wanted Sea Monkeys. We all remember the Kennedy assassination, the moon landing, Watergate... Television served as a great unifier for our generation, and because of it, we all have a lot of the same "nostalgia buttons," which get pushed when we see certain objects. Like a chrome dinette, a Pet Rock, or a peace symbol.

That is why this book is so cool. It pushes our nostalgia buttons to the point of overload. But, beyond that, it is a valuable tool to show us that, because of the way we cherish our past, collectibles from the 50s, 60s and 70s have escalated in value faster than those from any decade before. Because we place such value on our childhood memories (and many of us are actively buying them back) these pop culture artifacts have taken on staggering worth in some cases.

In the business of buying and selling 50s, 60s and 70s merchandise, nothing gives us more satisfaction than hearing phrases like "I had that!" or "Oh my gosh, my old lunchbox!" It tells us that our customers appreciate what we have done. They like the fact that we have rediscovered bits of their past, rescued them from garage sales and flea markets, uncovered them in thrift stores and basements. Pop culture archaeologists, we dig and discover, carefully dusting off the bones of our childhoods, preserving and presenting important artifacts for others to cherish.

It makes us feel good. It makes our customers feel good. We hope this book will make you feel good, as you leaf through its pages of memory-jogging photos and say, "I had that!" and "I remember these!"

There are two kinds of people who buy 50s, 60s and 70s stuff: the nostalgic impulse buyer, and the serious collector. Often, the serious collector began, innocently enough, as a nostalgic impulse buyer. But like many from our generation, soon found that the nostalgia rush from one lunchbox led to the purchase of another and another, and soon he was curious about the hard stuff. He began buying back his GI Joe dolls and Marx figures, and before long, he was purchasing entire playsets, sometimes even mint in box.

Like any addict, he realized his habit was expensive, he knew he was becoming obsessed. His friends began to wonder about his priorities. But he didn't care. He had become a serious collector.

Here's hoping you do the same. And, have a nice day.

Dana Cain
Atomic Antiques & Collectibles
Denver, Colorado

WHAT'S COOKIN' IN THE KITCHEN

Few things in life are as charming as a well-done 1950s style kitchen. Polished chrome and colorful vintage formica brighten up the home and are easily enhanced by the wide availability of nostalgic kitchen accessories. Some of the more popular color themes: red and white; pink and black; aqua and yellow, gray and anything. If a decorator doesn't mind mixing decades, nothing is quite as cheery as a yellow chrome dinette accented with "Happy Face" accessories such as a wall clock, the McCoy Happy Face cookie jar, etc.

Chrome dinettes commonly sell for $175-$400, depending on the color and condition. Ripped vinyl chairs is a common problem, and sets with the original vinyl in good condition typically bring the highest prices. Gray and yellow sets seem to be the easiest to find, although red, aqua and pink are the most desirable. Pink chrome dinette sets are very tough to find, and command the very highest prices.

For a more 1970s look, think "mushrooms." If your refrigerator and dishwasher are avocado green or harvest gold; if your counter tops are orange or brown, you have the beginnings of a great 1970s kitchen. Buy mushroom canisters and a round dinette set. A few daisies in a brown jug and you're set.

COLLECTIBLE KITCHEN ACCESSORIES

Salt and pepper shakers and cookie jars are among the most collectible of all kitchen accessories, boasting thousands of collectors from coast to coast. Some collect only crystal or cut glass salt and peppers (S&P). Others go for the figural S&P sets, or the animated ones. S&P sets are easily found at antique shows or collectibles shops, and always brighten their surroundings with color, fun and variety. Another big bonus for this type of collection is that prices are still very reasonable. Good S&P sets typically cost $8-30, with a few notable exceptions.

Cookie jars, on the other hand, can cost big bucks. Some "Mammy" cookie jars from the 1950s command hundreds of dollars, and are hunted by collectors of cookie jars and Black memorabilia alike. Vintage Disney cookie jars are also quite valuable. A nice collection of ceramic cookie jars looks quite impressive when displayed on a rustic wooden shelf in a 1950s style kitchen!

COOKBOOKS

Even as we near the 21st century, enjoying the zenith of the fast food drive-thru age, some people continue to buy groceries and cook their own food. It is from this wholesome segment of the population that most of today's cookbook collectors are generated. They collect for the recipes, primarily, searching for tasty dishes that have been forgotten or overlooked, the obscure, remote and delicious.

Cookbooks are also collectible if they were a give-away from a certain product, such as JELL-O or Campbell's Soup. Also, catchy titles, covers and celebrity tie-ins add to a cookbook's collectibility.

Today, certain companies are publishing cookbooks primarily for the collectibles market. In 1993, actress Dawn Wells issued Mary Ann's Gilligan's Island Cookbook, a very hot seller filled with tropical recipes, cast photos and dialogue blurbs from the ever-popular TV show!

THE HAPPY HOUR HOSTESS

Bar and cocktail accessories were an important component of a well-appointed home in the 1950s and 60s. Cocktail parties were huge in the late 1950s and early 60s, and a well-stocked, well-detailed bar area was a must for "the hostess with the mostess." Ice crushers, shakers, jiggers, stirrers, swizzle sticks, ice buckets and, of course, the right glassware were needed.

Today, many of these items seem passe, and some are so passe and dated that they are collectible, too!

Mushroom ceramic wall clock. 1970s. $20-30.

Mushroom large canister and small canister. 1970s. $20-30 set.

Mushroom ceramic canister set on swivel base. 1970s. $40-50.

Mushroom ceramic stubby salt and pepper set. 1970s. $8-10.

Mushroom ceramic tall salt and pepper
set. 1970s. $7-10.

Set of 4 bowls with mushrooms painted
inside. 1970s. $4-5 each.

Set of 4 mushroom glasses. 1970s. $16-20
set.

Set of 4 plates with painted mushrooms. 1970s. $18-22.

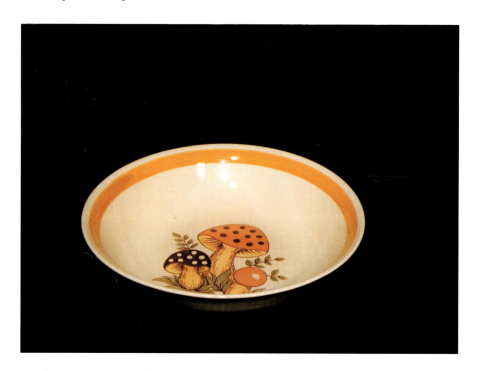

Mushroom bowl. 1970s. $10-15.

Cotton place mat with mushrooms. 1970s. $20-25 set.

Metal bread box decorated with mushrooms. 1970s. $35-45.

Floral drinking glasses. 1950s. $2-3 each.

Set of glasses in a metal rack. 1950s-60s. $10-15.

Glass floral bowl. 1950s. $10-15.

Gold dot casserole dish in metal frame. 1950s-60s. $20-25.

Glass batter bowl with painted on leaf arrangement. 1950s. $8-10.

Set of 3 oven proof bowls. 1960s. $25-30.

Set of 4 oven proof bowls. 1950s. $40-50 set.

Metal red and floral cake carrier. 1950s. $20-25.

Brown floral cake carrier, metal. 1950s-60s. $10-12.

Metal floral cake carrier. 1950s-60s. $8-10.

Aluminum cake carrier by Regal. 1960s. $10-20.

Tin cake carrier with metal handle. 1950s. $8-12.

Metal and tin floral cake carrier. 1950s-60s. $12-15.

Aluminum stacking canister set. 1970s. $20-25 set.

Set of 4 aluminum canisters. 1960s. $30-40.

Aluminum 7 piece canister set with plastic lids. 1960s. $40-50.

Ceramic 4 piece revolving canister set with wooden top. 1950s. $100-125.

Wooden hand painted canister set. 1960s. $30-40.

Tin 4 piece canister set with flowers. 1950s-60s. $15-20.

Ceramic spice set in wooden rack. 1950s-60s. $10-15.

Wooden spice rack with spices. 1960s. $20-30.

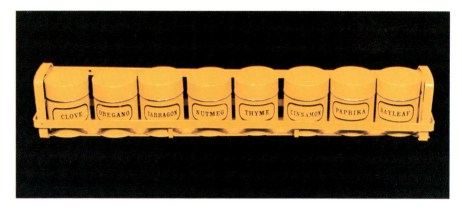

Tin yellow spice rack and spices. 1970s. $25-35.

Wooden rack with ceramic spices. 1950s-60s. $20-25.

Metal spice set in rack. 12" x 3". 1960s. $12-15.

China candy dish hand painted and signed by "Erica". 1950s. $15-20.

China ashtrays hand painted and signed by "Erica". 1950s. $25-35.

China cigarette dish signed "Erica".
1950s. $20-25.

Electric hot plate hand painted and
signed by Georges Briard. 1950-1960s.
$30-40.

Glass meat serving dish. 1950s-60s. $8-
10.

Ceramic tea pot. 1960. $20-25.

Ceramic tea pot with fruit motif. 1950s-60s. $20-30.

"Tea time" ceramic tea pot. 1960s. $20-25.

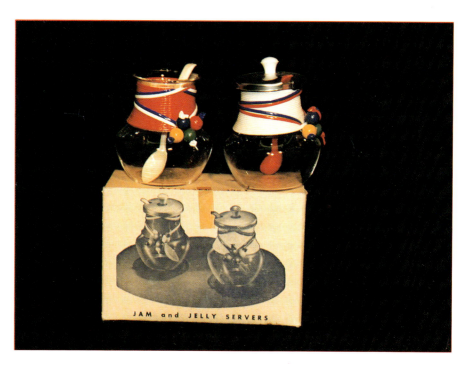

Jam and jelly glass servers by Weico. 1960s. $20-25.

Holiday glass servettes by Weico. 1960s. $15-20.

Fiberglass floral salad bowl set. 1950s. $15-20 set.

Fiberglass floral serving dish with metal handle. 11". 1950s. $10-15.

Three piece set, bowl and candle holders. 1950s. $20-30.

Ceramic lobster bowl with side dishes and salt and pepper set. California Pottery Co. $150-175 set.

Glass Lazy Susan with brass holder. 1950s. $30-40.

Glidden Pottery Lazey Daisy. 1960s-70s. $75-100.

Fish-shaped ceramic Lazy Susan dish. 1950s. $40-50.

Aluminum two-tier candy tray. 1950s-60s. $10-15.

Pottery Lazy Susan on metal swivel. 1960s-70s. $20-30.

Glidden Pottery poodle dishes. 1960s-70s. $35-45.

Aluminum jelly jar with cranberry glass bowl and spoon. $25-35.

Pink ceramic covered candy dish. "Gilner". 1950s. $15-20.

Ceramic cracker jar with hand painted rooster on front and wicker handle. 1960s. $40-50.

Wooden knife holder. 1950s-60s. $8-10.

Wooden match holder. 1960s. $15-20.

Wooden knife holder and shopping reminder. 1950s. $10-15.

Wooden popcorn bowl with handle.
1960s. $8-10.

Wooden potato chip bowl with handle.
1960s. $8-10.

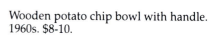

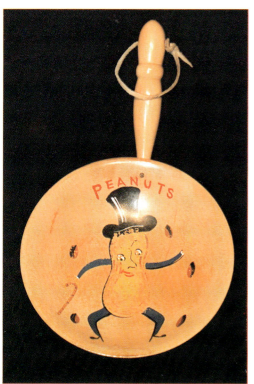

Wooden nut bowl with handle. 1960s.
$8-10.

Wooden recipe box with decals of a carrot and corn. 1970s. $10-15.

Tin recipe box with black floral trim by Ohio Art Co. 1960s. $8-10.

Tin floral recipe box. 1950s. $5-7.

Tin recipe box from Ohio Art Co. 1960s.
$8-10.

Tin recipe box from Hallmark. 1970s.
$10-15.

Metal recipe box. 1950s. $6-10.

Wooden recipe box. 1970s. $10-12.

Metal serving tray. 1960s. $10-15.

Metal serving tray. 1960s. $10-15.

Metal serving tray. 1960s. $10-15.

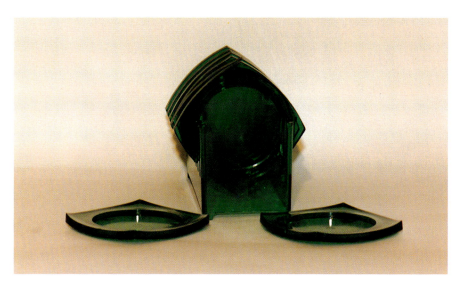

Plastic coaster set in rack. 1960s. $10-15.

Metal napkin dispensers. 1960s. $20-25 each.

Plastic cream and sugar set. 1960s. $5-8.

Russell Wright spun aluminum bun warmer. 1960s. $60-70.

Forged aluminum casserole. 1960s-70s. $30-40.

Forged aluminum serving tray. 1960s-70s. $9-12.

Forged aluminum "Everlast" serving tray. 1960s- 70s. $13-15.

Stainless steal thermos pitcher. 1970s. $35-45.

Corning Glass coffee maker with plastic lid. 1960s-1970s. $20-30.

Brown pottery pitcher and mug set by Marcrest. 1970s. $30-40 set.

Chrome Craft coffee server with Bakelite handles. 1950s. $30-40.

Ceramic apple cookie jar by California Pottery. 1970s. $30-35.

Wooden silverware box with one drawer. 1950s. $30-40.

Aluminum quart pitcher with metal handle by Dura Ware. 1960s. $20-25.

Aluminum quart pitcher with plastic handle by Dura Ware. 1960s. $10-15.

Metal serving tray with glass insert and floral design under the glass. 11" x 18". 1960s. $25-30.

Enamel coffee pot with cups, with graphics by Georges Briard. Base holds candle for warming. 1960s. $70-85.

Aluminum quart pitcher with brass handle by Dura Ware. 1960s. $20-25.

Servemaster ice bucket with plastic
inlay. 7". 1950s-60s. $8-10.

Servemaster ice basket with metal inlay.
7". 1950s. $15-20.

Four piece martini set in brass wire rack. 1970s. $30-40.

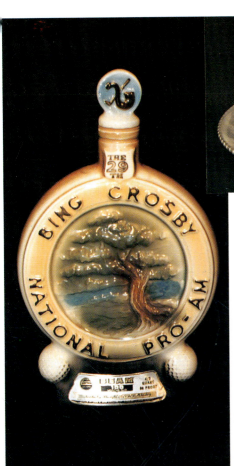

Aluminum candy tray by Farberware. 1950s-60s. $8-10.

Jim Beam liquor bottle from the 29th Bing Crosby National Pro-Am golf tournament. 1970s. $10-15.

Pee Wee ashtrays. Set of three in original box. 1970s. $10-15.

Swirl glass candy dish. 1970s. $30-40.

Mosaic tile ashtray. 1970s. $10-15.

Pair of resin hot plates with colored glass inserts. 1970s. $20-30.

Plaid metal picnic cooler. 1950s. $18-22.   Plaid metal picnic cooler. 1950s. $15-20.

Plaid metal picnic basket with thermos and hooks to hang on car seat. 1950s. $20-30.

Aluminum ice bucket with green ceramic liner. 1960s. $10-15.

Metal glass lined cooler, red with white polka dots. 1960s. $20-30.

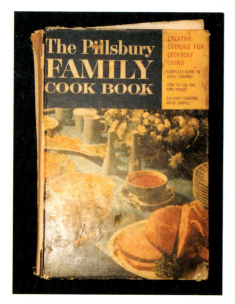

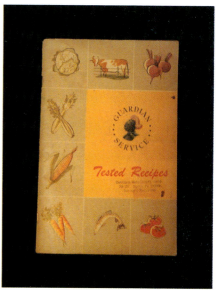

The Pillsbury Family Cook Book. 1969. $15-18.

Guardian Service Tested Recipes. 1960. $5-8.

FURNISHINGS AND HOME DECOR

Color was very important in the 1950s, 1960s and early 1970s. Today, sometimes all it takes is a color to peg an item as being manufactured during the time frame. A pink or aqua chrome dinette could only be from the 1950s. If a chair is avocado green, chances are it is a product of the early 1970s. Bright orange vinyl - probably late 1960s. Hot pink plastic - definitely 60s. The vintage 50s, 60s and 70s colors were wonderful - right up until people shifted to "Earth Tones" in the mid-1970s. Then it was bye-bye purple shag carpet, hello brown mottled look. Oh, well.

Today, there is a growing market for Brady Bunch-style home decor. There is a certain audience that actually craves shag carpet and molded plastic chairs. Macrame owls are getting harder to find in thrift stores.

But, when it comes to home decor, the 1950s is THE decade. Stylish modern designs by Heywood Wakefield, Herman Miller, Eames and others can bring incredible prices. Collectors and interior decorators crave the amoeba-shaped end tables, boomerang coffee tables, fringed sectional sofas and ultra-modern accessories.

MEET GEORGE JETSON...AND HIS COUCH

Two of the most popular styles of post-war vintage furniture are modern and western. If it looks like it came out of George Jetson's house, or out of Roy Rogers' ranch, its cool.

The spacey Jetsons look is represented by a number of 1950s, 60s and 70s manufacturers, and has been created from a variety of materials. Bent wood is very collectible, and some chairs command more than $500 each. Upholstered boomerang-shaped sofas and coffee tables, issued in the 1950s are always in high demand, and consequently, sell for top dollar in good condition. In the late 1960s and early 1970s, chairs, sofas and tables made of molded fiberglass in bold solid colors were introduced, as were the incredible inflatable furniture pieces. Inflatable furniture is very hard to find today, and, because of its "puncturability," is considered a great find in good condition.

WAY OUT WESTERN

Western furniture and home accents have become very popular in the 1990s. During the 1950s, some really fun western furniture was created from ranch oak and Naugahyde, which, today, is extremely collectible. Some of the best finds of this type of furniture have come from small hotels dotting the western plains. Typically, a sofa and matching rocking chair were decorated with vinyl cutouts sewn onto the back depicting a horse head, a cowboy on a bucking bronco, or a saddle. The couch and chair featured ranch oak arms, sometimes with a wagon wheel design which was carried over into the ranch oak coffee table and end tables. The most desirable sets are heavy, with two-toned wood and red vinyl, and sell for $1000-$1500. Sets were also issued in tan, cream and green.

Outside of living room sets, western bedrooms (especially for little boys) were very popular in the 1950s and early 1960s. Consequently, a number of cowboy bedspreads, coat racks and bureaus were manufactured. The most collectible are the big-name cowboy items (especially Hopalong Cassidy and Roy Rogers). A Roy Rogers bedspread is worth $150-175 today.

Bamboo sofa by Heywood Wakefield, with cloth cushions. 1960s. $225-300.

Boomerang couch by Futorian Company. 1950s. $600-700.

Bamboo breakfast bar. 1970s. $200-275.

Oak table with vinyl covered chairs. 1950s- 60s. $400-500.

Child's walker-table with formica top. 1950s. $50-75.

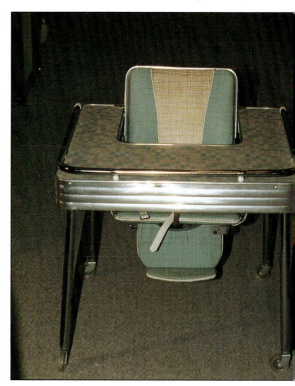

Vinyl covered arm chair and ottoman with stainless steel legs. 1960s. $175-200.

Cone chair. Black vinyl designed by Verner Panton. 1950s. $1,300-1,400.

Pair of orange nylon-covered chairs. 1950s. $125-150 each.

Woven mesh and wood chair. 1960s-70s. $60-70.

Vinyl covered chair with wrought iron legs. 1960s. $75-100.

Upholstered arm chair. 1960s. $200-275.

Upholstered chair with wooden arms. 1960s-70s. $200-300.

Metal frame and plastic covered seat,
bar stool. 1950s-60s. $50-60.

Vinyl stool with stainless swivel base
and wood trim. 1970s. $100-125.

Steel leg vinyl covered stools. 1950s. $200-300.

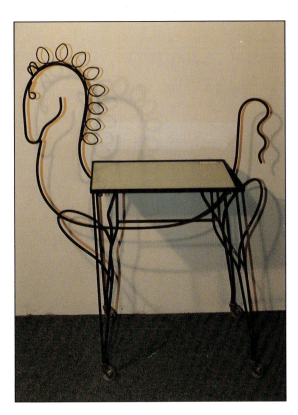

Pony wrought iron serving cart with glass top. 1950s. $250-275.

Ceramic lamp with plastic scenic shade. 1960s. $45-55.

Heywood Wakefield (knock off?) oak end table. 1960s. $75-100.

Heywood Wakefield Pouffe reupholstered stool. 1950s-60. $150-175.

Herman Miller end table by George Nelson. 1950s. $275-300.

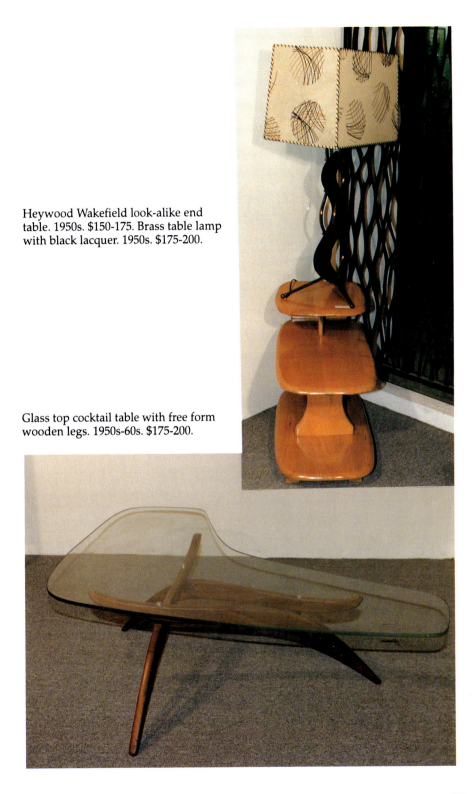

Heywood Wakefield look-alike end table. 1950s. $150-175. Brass table lamp with black lacquer. 1950s. $175-200.

Glass top cocktail table with free form wooden legs. 1950s-60s. $175-200.

Pair of gumwood kidney shaped end tables with brass leg caps. 1950s-60s. $300-350 pair.

Formica coffee table with wood legs. 1950s. $125-150.

Round blond coffee table with brass leg caps. 1950s. $40-50.

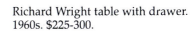

Wood telephone stand with storage for phone book. 1950s-60s. $40-50.

Richard Wright table with drawer. 1960s. $225-300.

Vinyl covered storage stool. 1960s-70s.
$75-100.

Wrought iron magazine holder. 1960s-
70s. $15-20.

Three stacking vinyl covered stools.
1960s. $30-40.

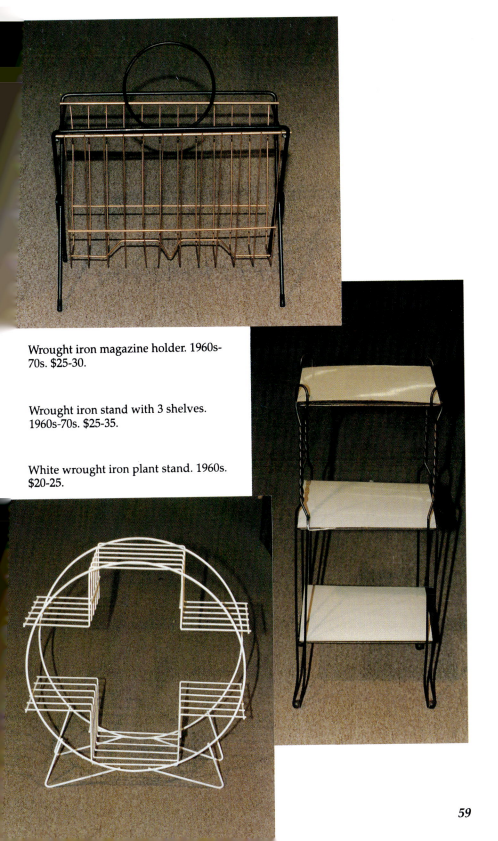

Wrought iron magazine holder. 1960s-
70s. $25-30.

Wrought iron stand with 3 shelves.
1960s-70s. $25-35.

White wrought iron plant stand. 1960s.
$20-25.

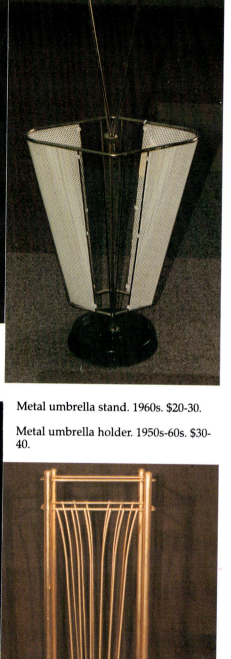

Metal plant holder. 1960s. $30-40.

Metal umbrella stand with plastic insert. 1950s. $20-30.

Metal umbrella stand. 1960s. $20-30.

Metal umbrella holder. 1950s-60s. $30-40.

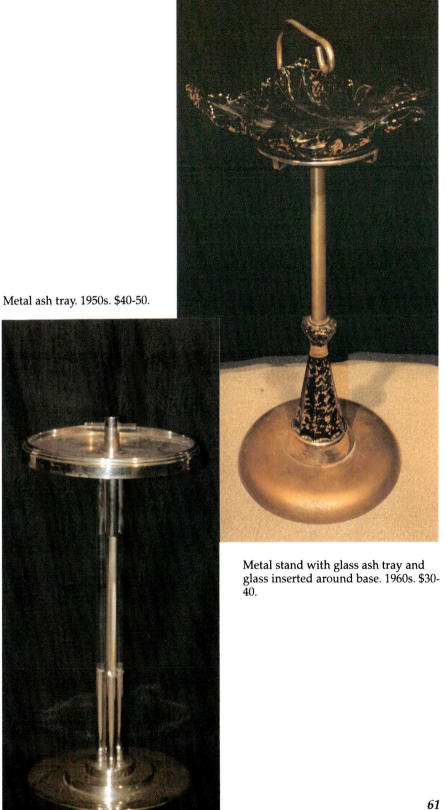

Metal ash tray. 1950s. $40-50.

Metal stand with glass ash tray and glass inserted around base. 1960s. $30-40.

Wooden sewing box. 1950s. $30-40.

Pagoda style table lamp. Fiberglass shade, wood and brass base. 1960s. $25-35.

Ash tray metal with a glass "Hull" ashtray. 1960s. $20-25.

Chalk poodle T.V. lamp. 1950s. $50-60.

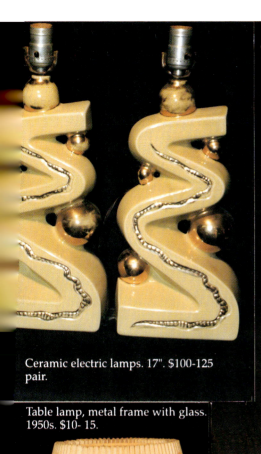

Ceramic electric lamps. 17". $100-125 pair.

Ceramic lamp with fiberglass shade. 26". 1950s. $40-50.

Table lamp, metal frame with glass. 1950s. $10- 15.

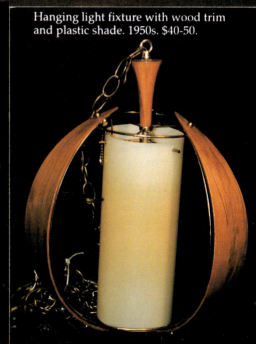

Hanging light fixture with wood trim and plastic shade. 1950s. $40-50.

Lamp table with plastic shades and marble look shelf and top. 1950s. $150-200.

Poppy Trail table lamp by Metlox. 1960s. $100-125.

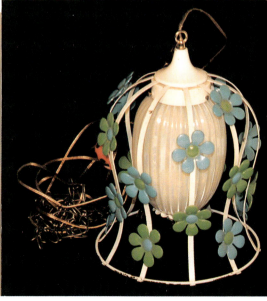

Wrought iron table lamp with fiberglass shade. 1950s. $40-50.

Wrought iron hanging light with metal flowers. 1960s. $60-75.

Metal lighthouse lamp. 1950-60s. $100-125.

Ceramic boat lamp with tin sails. 1950s. $70-80.

Brass boot light. 1960s-70s. $15-20.

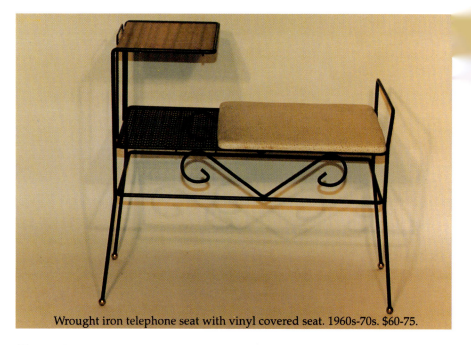

Wrought iron telephone seat with vinyl covered seat. 1960s-70s. $60-75.

Glass and brass wall light fixture. 1950s. $15- 20.

AM/FM Multibox Bubble Radio with 8 track stereo by Welton. $120-140.

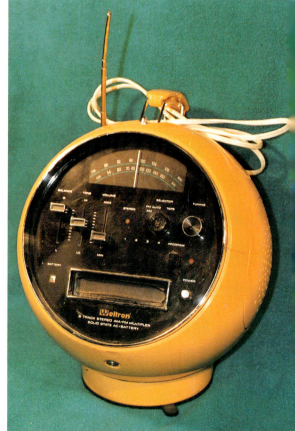

Metal T.V. clock by United. 1960s. $20-25.

Metal and turquoise plastic General Electric table model television with 8" screen. 1950s. $150-175.

Silver Panasonic bubble television set with 5" screen. 1950s. $150-200.

Telechrome alarm clock with brass frame. 1960s. $50-60.

Oscar the Grouch Talking Alarm Clock from Sesame Street by Milton Bradley. 1977. $35-35.

Turquoise plastic desk phone. 1960s-70s. $30-40.

Pictures of girl and boy. 16.5" x 22.5". 1960s. $20-30 set.

Wooden framed pictures by Pabi. 5 1/2" x 7 1/2". 1950s. $4-5 pair.

Chalk fruit wall hanger. 1950s. $5-8.

Chalk bird wall hanger and thermometer. 1950s. $10-15.

Ceramic big eye dog. 1960s. $8-12.

Ceramic cat figure with fur. Japan. 1950s. $8-10.

Ceramic soldier figurine by Walls. Japan. 1950s. $10-15.

Ceramic owl wallpocket. 1950s-60s. $10-15.

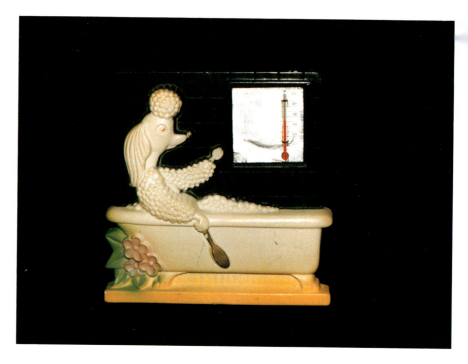

Chalk poodle wall hanger and thermometer. 1950s. $10-15.

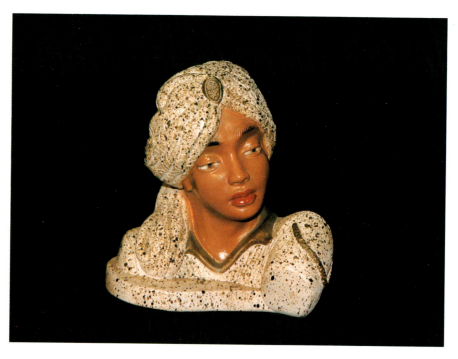

Chalk bust of India male. 1950s. $35-40.

Chrome wall plaques in the shape of bottles. 1950s. $30-40.

Blue plastic flowers on plastic base. 1960s-70s. $15-20.

Bronze horse book ends. 4" x 6". 1960s. $75-100 pair.

Abingdon horse book ends. 7". $100-125.

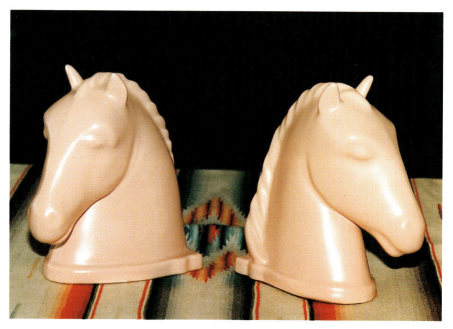

Chalk horses on a horse shoe wall hanger. 7". 1960s. $25-35.

Stone art business card holder. 1960s-70s. $25-35.

Breyer plastic Arabian high gloss horse. Mid-60s. 9" x 10". $25-35.

Breyer plastic Clydesdale and foal with matte finish. 1970s. 10" x 11" large horse. 8" x 8" foal. $30- 40 pair.

Hartland mare and foal. 1960s. 5" x 6" mare. 3" x 3 1/2" foal. $12-18 pair.

Paper mache turtle bank. 5". Holiday
Fair. 1971. $7-10.

Paper mache purple elephant bank. 6 1/
2". Japan. 1970. $8-12.

Paper mache tiger bank. 7". Taiwan.
1970s. $8-12.

Paper mache pink elephant bank. 7".
Japan. 1969. $8-12.

Paper mache floral kitten bank. 7".
Lego-Japan. 1970. $7-10.

Gold ceramic with blue base marked "China 44". 6" x 6". $40-50.

Wooden cat set. 8"and 5". 1960s. $20-25 set.

Plastic black "Groove On Brother." 1950s-60s. $6-10.

Wood and metal cat and mouse letter holder. 4". 1960s. $8-10.

Metal bird cage. 1950s. $15-20.

Brass wall candle holder for 4 candles. 1960s. $25-30.

Metal poodle waste paper basket. 1950s-60s. $10-15.

Pink cotton and rhinestone pillow.
1970s. $30-40.

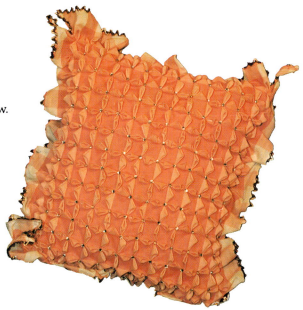

Vohann of California ceramic covered
box. 1960s. 3.5" x 8". $15-20.

Anchorettes by Georges Briard. 1950s-
60s. $15- 20.

Dritz plastic skirt marker in original box. 1950s. $8-10.

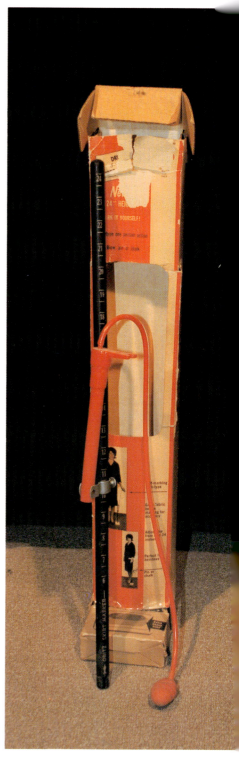

Wicker sewing basket with satin lining. 1960s. $15-20.

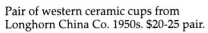

Pair of western ceramic cups from Longhorn China Co. 1950s. $20-25 pair.

China western bowl with wooden handle from Longhorn China Co. 1950s. $15-20.

China western napkin holder from Longhorn China Co. 1950s. $20-30.

Western enameled coffee pot. 1950s-60s. $35-45.

Western ceramic pitcher by Tyger Pottery. 1950s- 60s. $50-60.

Set of western glasses in a wood rack. 1950s. $30-40.

Ceramic western cup by E.O. Brody, Cleveland, Ohio, made in Japan. 1960s. $20-25.

Wooden western salt and pepper set. 1950s-60s. $8-10.

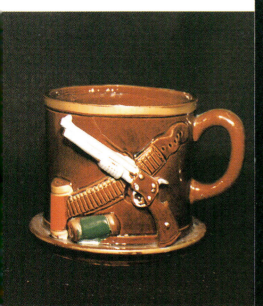

Western ceiling light fixture. 1950s. $30-40.

Satin glass cocktail shaker with western motif. 1950s. $25-30.

Cardboard advertising for Weather-Bird cowboy boots. 1950s-60s. $30-40.

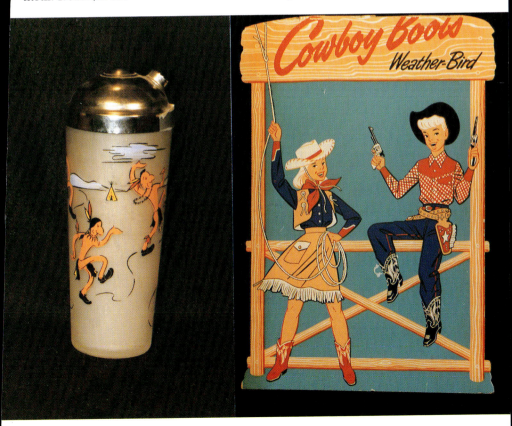

TV AND MOVIE COLLECTIBLES

Many collectors believe the golden age of television was the 1960s. And lots of today's most collectible shows were aired during that decade, including, of course, the most collectable TV show of all time - Star Trek.

STAR TREK: INVEST NOW & PROSPER

Memorabilia issued during the show's initial run in the mid-1960s is rare and highly sought by today's Star Trek collectors. The domed steel lunchbox and thermos kit sells for about $700-1100; the large metal and plastic Dinky brand Enterprise sells for $225 mint in box; the first Star Trek TV Guide cover issued is valued at over $150; The original #1 Gold Key Star Trek Comic Book guides at more than $350.

Most of the first Star Trek memorabilia was actually issued in the 1970s, just before Paramount decided to release Star Trek: The Motion Picture, and after fans of the show had had nearly a decade to coalesce into the greatest TV fan force in history - the Trekkies (or Trekkers as some prefer to be called).

Today, one study showed that roughly half of all U.S. residents consider themselves fans of Star Trek, and Paramount's Star Trek "franchise" has built a successful track record of releasing a string of new movies and TV series. New Star Trek toys and memorabilia have flooded the market, and several stores and businesses are dedicated to merchandising and selling only Star Trek items. This is one collectible arena that seems to be a risk-free investment idea. And, naturally, the original merchandise, issued in the 60s and 70s, is the most prized of all. Prices for vintage Trek memorabilia are assured to escalate well into the coming century.

SCIENCE FICTION, FANTASY & HORROR

Star Trek is not the only hot show to emerge from the 50s, 60s and 70s, in terms of collectibility. Many of the other science fiction and horror-oriented shows from the period have grown a cult following. Lost in Space, which made its debut in 1963, produced a variety of great collectibles, including several versions of the Robot. At a recent toy auction, in fact, a Lost in Space gun sold for more than $14,000, reportedly the highest toy price ever paid.

Also very collectible are: The Outer Limits, The Twilight Zone, Land of the Giants, Voyage to the Bottom of the Sea, The Munsters, The Addams Family, Battlestar Galactica, Dark Shadows and Dr. Who (British). In fact, the only science fiction from the period which no one seems interested in is It's About Time. Oh, well.

Aside from Star Trek, the most collected TV show from the 60s is probably Batman, the campy version of DC's superhero brought to life on the small screen by Adam West and his faithful companion Burt Ward (Robin). Today, Batman's popularity is greater than ever, thanks to the revamping of his legend in the comics and on the big screen. But for many, Adam West is Batman and nothing before or since can compare to his version of the caped crusader. The Batman TV Show produced a plethora of wonderful collectibles in the 1960s, including several renditions of the Batmobile, great cover shots on *Life* and *TV Guide*, board games, costumes, Mego figures and much more.

OTHER COLLECTIBLE TV SHOWS

Some of the most valuable collectibles to come out of the 50s, 60s and 70s resulted from popular situation comedies and family shows of the times. Among the hottest today are: The Brady Bunch, The Partridge Family, Welcome Back Kotter, The Dukes of Hazzard, Gilligan's Island, Mr. Ed, I Dream of Jeannie, The Andy Griffith Show, Lassie and anything starring Lucille Ball. The earlier shows, such as Andy Griffith, didn't feature much in the way of merchandising in the 1960s. Consequently, anything found is valuable.

By the 70s, however, many of the popular sitcoms featured teen idols, which, in turn, meant more merchandising. And the networks knew their markets. Subsequently, you can now buy vintage paper dolls of Fonzie (Henry Winkler on Happy Days) and Vinnie Barbarino (John Travolta, Welcome Back Kotter). Lunch boxes were issued, as were paperback novels and all sorts of other items.

Saturday morning was a special time in the 1950s, 60s and 70s, and the kids who sat entranced in front of the TV then are eager to buy related merchandise today. Hanna-Barbera seems to be the biggest seller, as a huge collectors base has built up around the Jetsons, the Flintstones, Huckleberry Hound, Yogi and others. Atom Ant, Space Ghost and Scooby-Doo are hot, as are virtually all of the early British and Japanese import "kid-vid" (Fireball XL-5, Thunderbirds, Supercar; Astro Boy, Gigantor, Speed Racer).

Also prized are items relating to Howdy Doody, Sesame Street, The Mickey Mouse Club, Captain Kangaroo and, to a lesser extent, Shari Lewis.

THE SILVER SCREEN

Movie collecting is a fast-growing hobby today, focusing primarily in the areas of promotional one-sheets, lobby cards, autographs, props and licensed merchandise such as toys and dolls.

Original movie posters and lobby cards from the 1950s-70s were never intended for public sale and were limited to copies printed for display at public theaters. The idea was that companies would display the poster to promote the film and then mail it back to the distributor or toss it out. Luckily, it didn't always happen that way, and today, these posters and cards, although sometimes tough to find, can be found and purchased, for a price. While the classic movie posters from the 20s, 30s and 40s often sell for astronomical prices, many titles from the 60s and 70s are still dirt cheap, often under $25. These can be great investments, especially if the collector focuses on a genre like science fiction, horror or counterculture, where the audience is guaranteed. The main things to look for in a movie poster are: 1) The graphic image. Is it frameable? Will it look good on the wall? 2) The title. Have you heard of the movie? Was it popular? Will anyone care? and 3) The stars. Even if it was a dumb movie, if it starred Jayne Mansfield, Liz Taylor, Elvis or John Travolta, it's got investment potential, and it's collectible.

STAR WARS: MAY THE CHECKBOOK BE WITH YOU

Of all the movies released in the 50s, 60s and 70s, the one that has sparked the biggest collecting frenzy is undoubtedly Star Wars. Sure, the Star Trek movie is up there, but its success was owed to the TV series, not that first film. Planet of the Apes also enjoys a large collector following, and there's lots of great ape merchandise to collect, too.

But nothing really comes close to Star Wars. A good Star Wars collection can fill one or two rooms, a whole basement or an entire house. Although some of the merchandise wasn't issued until the sequels appeared in the 1980s, the Star Wars phenomenon began in 1977.

Many Star Wars collectors focus exclusively on the action figures, vehicles and their accessories. Some prefer to buy these toys loose, because they actually enjoy playing with them. Of course, the most valuable Star Wars pieces are those that are still mint on mint card/box. Among the rarest Star Wars action figures: Han Solo in Carbonite; Blue Snaggletooth and Yak Face, all of which command $80-$125 loose!

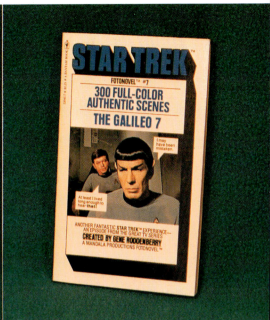

Star Trek phaser saucer gun by Ahi. 1976. $50-60.

Star Trek Fotonovel #7: The Galileo Seven from Bantam. 1978. $20-25.

Star Trek Fotonovel #4: A Taste of Armageddon from Bantam. 1978. $15-20.

Star Trek communicators, walkie talkies from Mego. 1974. $100-125.

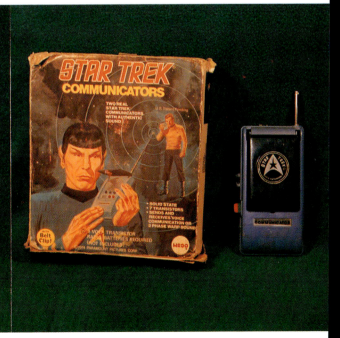

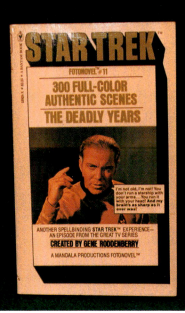

Star Trek Fotonovel #11: The Deadly Years from Bantam. 1978. $20-25.

Star Trek poseable figure on original card from Mego. Spock. 1979. $25-35.

Star Trek Fotonovel #12: Amok Time from Bantam. 1978. $30-40.

Star Trek poseable figure on original card from Mego. Captain Kirk. 1979. $20-25.

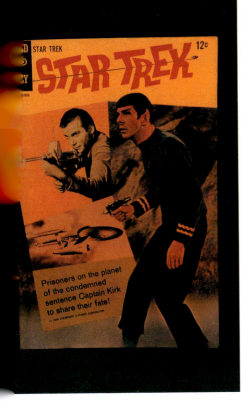

Star Trek #2 comic from Gold Key. 1968. $80-100.

Star Trek poseable figure on original card from Mego. Ilia. 1979. $40-50.

Star Trek #3 comic from Gold Key. 1968. $40-50.

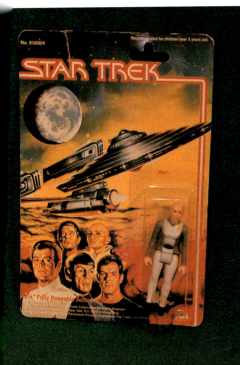

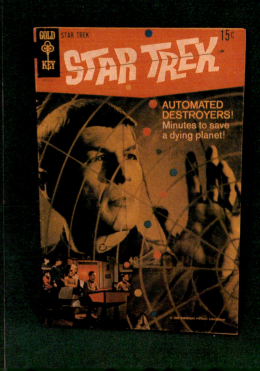

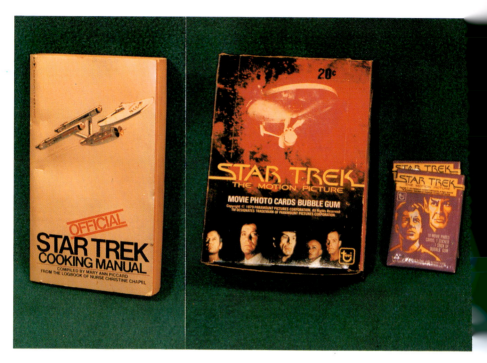

Official Star Trek Cooking Manual from
Bantam. 1978. $20-30.

Star Trek trading cards from "Star Trek:
The Motion Picture." Topps in original
wax box. 1979. $80-100. Box $5- 8.

Star Trek U.S.S. Enterprise by Dinkie Co. Metal and plastic. 1976. $125-150.

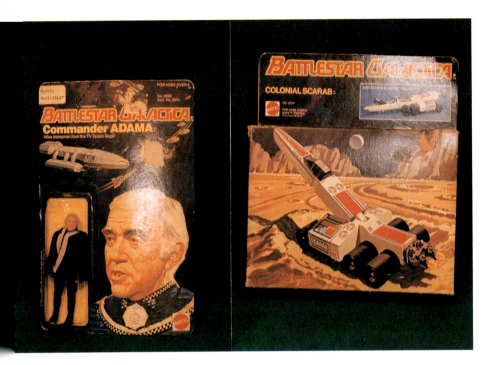

Battlestar Galactica Commander Adama figurine. Mattel. 1978. $30-40.

Colonial Scarab from Battlestar Galactica. Mattel. 1978. $35-45.

The Official Battlestar Galactica Blueprints. Today Press. 1978. $20-30.

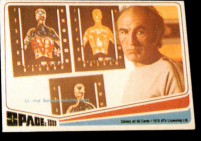

Space: 1999 trading cards by Donruss, 1976. $.50-1.00 each.

24 – Eagle I preparing to land.

56 – Alpha astronauts calculate speed of runaway Moon.

30 – Comdr. Koenig's brain is probed as his companions look on helplessly.

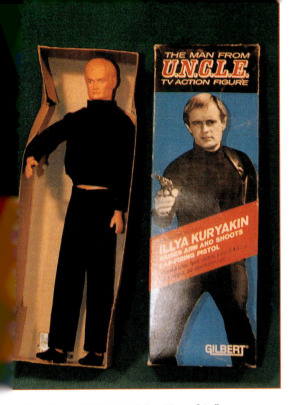

Man from U.N.C.L.E. "Illya Kuryakin" doll by Gilbert. 1965. 12". $180-200.

John Travolta Superstar doll. Chemtoy. 1977. 12". $35-45.

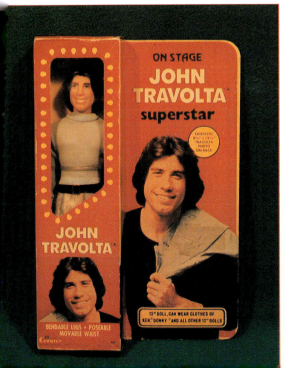

Welcome Back Kotter "Barbarino" doll by Mattel. 1976. 11". $30-40.

Happy Days Fonzie Paper Doll. 1976. $20-30.

Patty Duke paper dolls by Whitman. 1965. $15-20.

Debbie Reynolds Cut-Outs, paper doll by Whitman. 1962. $25-35.

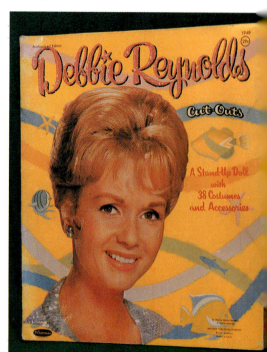

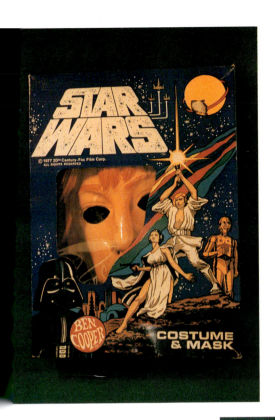

Luke Skywalker costume by Ben Cooper. 1977. $30-40.

Boba Fett doll in box by Kenner. 15". 1978. $180-200.

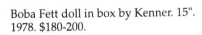

Plastic Luke Skywalker doll by Kenner. 1978. $125-150.

Plastic Patrol Dewback by Kenner. 11". 1977. $25-35.

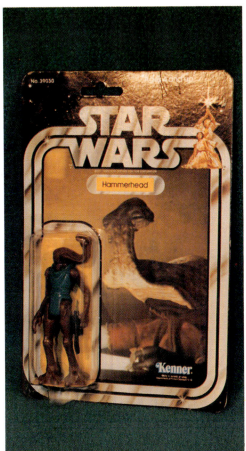

Hammerhead figure on card by Kenner. 4". 1977. $80-100.

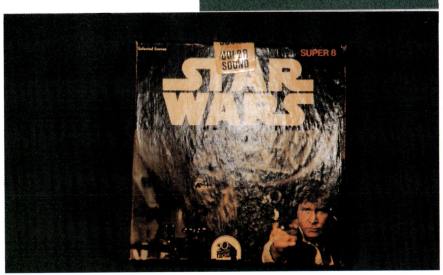

Star Wars super 6 film with selected scores by Ken films. 1977. $25-35.

Millenium Falcon, plastic by Kenner. 1977. $90-120.

Millenium Falcon from Kenner. Small die cast by Kenner. 1979. $40-50.

Star Wars watches by Texas Instruments. 1977. $90-110 each.

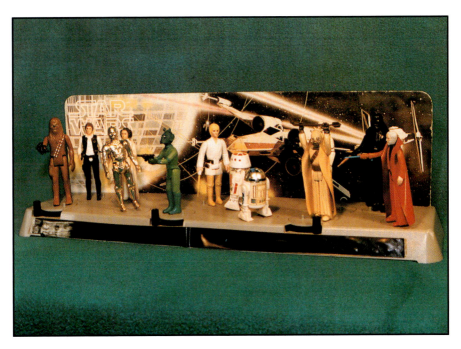

Star Wars figures with display by Kenner. 1977. Figures 4 1/4". Display 20" x 7". $200-250 set.

TOYS

Toys represent the single largest collectibles arena of the 50s, 60s and 70s. Why? The answer is simple. All of the Baby Boomers and many of the Generation Xers are buying back their old toys. Those kids are now the working population of America. And many choose to spend their disposable income reclaiming their childhood.

Consequently, the toys we wanted then are, for the most part, the toys we want now. Barbies, cap guns, GI Joes, Thingmakers and Hot Wheels are in hot demand today, as they were then. The "Holy Trinity" of toy makers from the era, Marx, Mego and Mattel, produced the bulk of the collectible toys during that time, followed by Hasbro, Ideal and a few others.

DOLLS & ACTION FIGURE ANCESTORS

The advent of the Barbie doll in the late 1950s was a major influence on all the dolls that followed. Certainly, there was still a market for baby dolls, but the 12-inch fashion doll was what girls really craved. And now, girls played with dolls well into junior high, long after baby dolls had lost their appeal. Now, Barbie could go out on dates with Ken, and GI Joe could come roaring around the corner in his Jeep, wrestle Ken to the ground and whisk Barbie off into the night. Yes, doll play had come a long way.

Barbie remains one of the most popular and valuable collectible toys of the era. Some Barbie collectors insist on only the pre-1966 dolls and clothes, while others specialize in the mod-era Barbie collectibles. Most serious Barbie collectors aren't interested in the late 1970s dolls and accessories, although, in time, these items will surely escalate in value.

While older Barbies can be extremely collectible and valuable, her friends, however, have not fared quite as well. Ken, Midge, Francie, Skipper and the rest of Barbie's pals have increased in value only a fraction of the percentage that Barbie herself has. In fact, lots of Barbie's old clothes are worth more than Ken.

Barbie collectors are also extremely picky about condition. If a doll's hair has been cut, it's worthless. If the hands or feet have been gnawed by you or your dog, forget it. If a vintage Barbie outfit doesn't include the shoes or the hat, the value plummets. Ideally, the doll's body should be free of marks, scuffs, color flaws. Then, you have something.

Many of the same guidelines apply to GI Joe, the first really successful "doll" for boys. Today, GI Joe collectors are quite prevalent, and have warranted an annual convention and their own collectors newsletter.

During the 1970s, GI Joes began to shrink, through a series of different experimental sizes, and they still exist today, quite successfully, in a standard small action figure format.

Other collectible dolls and figures from the 60s and 70s include: Liddle Kiddles, Trolls, Crissy, Chatty Cathy, Betsy Wetsy, and Archie Bunker's Grandson (Joey Stivic), the controversial first "physically correct male baby doll."

Dolls that more closely resembled the popular GI Joe format included several successful lines issued by Marx and Mego. Marx's Best of the West series, which included Johnny and Jane West, a few Indians, villains, horses and more, remains very popular among today's collectors. Mego, more prevalent in the 1970s, issued several very collectible lines of jointed figures, including comic book superheroes, Star Trek characters and an assortment of TV and movie-based characters.

CARS & OTHER VEHICLES:
GREAT THINGS DID COME IN SMALL PACKAGES

Mattel's Hot Wheels line, introduced in the late 1960s, has become one of the hottest toy collectibles of all time. Followed by Matchbox, Corgi, Tootsie, Johnny Lightning and Dinky, Hot Wheels leads the pack of Boomer-era toy car collectibles. Most collectible are the "red line" Hot Wheels, issued prior to 1977 and featuring red lines on the tires. Mint on card cars are especially sought after, as are certain color variations. Hot Wheels were commonly issued in a variety of colors, and today, collectors especially crave the rarer metallic pink and purple finishes. As with all 60s and 70s toys, collectors demand that the cars be complete and in good condition.

Corgi, a British diecast toy car manufacturer, is especially noted for releasing some highly collectible licensed TV and movie cars, including The Man From U.N.C.L.E. and James Bond cars with moving parts, a Monkeemobile including all four Monkees seated inside, a Batmobile, the Green Hornet's Black Beauty and several others. Almost all sell for more than $100, and quickly. Corgis today are worth more in Britain than in the U.S.

Toy trains released in the 1950s, primarily by Marx and Lionel, are extremely popular collectibles, although trains issued in the 60s and 70s have never achieved the popularity of pre-1960 train sets. Likewise, trucks, boats, airplanes and toy tractors from the 40s and 50s are far more collectible than those from the 60s and 70s.

Tonka trucks and vehicles from the 1950s and early 1960s still appeal strongly to collectors but beware of the yellow "Might Tonka" series issued in the 1970s. Its time has not yet come, and most of those values, even for the biggest trucks, remain below $25-$35.

THE GAMES PEOPLE PLAYED

Board game collecting seems to be an immature hobby. I don't mean people who collect them are immature, I mean the hobby has not fully come into its own. This means that: a) many really cool games are currently undervalued and b) buying them now might be a good idea.

Today, games from the 50s, 60s and 70s tend to sell because they are affiliated with a particular TV show, movie or character. The Charlie's Angels game always sells fast at $20-$30, and the rare and highly coveted Outer Limits game can easily bring $150-$200.

But an old Concentration game can sit forever. Aside from the TV, film and character tie-in games, the ones that sell are the ones that offer collectors the biggest nostalgia rush (vintage Candy Land or Chutes & Ladders) or classic games with older versions of the playing pieces - like Risk games with the wooden blocks, which easily sell for $40-50.

Activity games, such as Mattel's Thingmaker sets, are very popular today, and with the recent re-release of Creepy Crawlers and its companion sets, the world of Thingmakers has gained a new audience. Creepy Crawlers, Creeple Peeple, Fun Flowers, Fighting Men, Mini-Dragons, and the rare carded specialty molds are very collectible. Incidentally, the Plastigoop being issued today can be used with the old-style molds and cookers!

THERE AIN'T NO SUCH THING AS A FREE LUNCH BOX

Lunch box collecting has become a popular hobby in the U.S. since the mid-1980s, and now supports its own newsletter and annual convention. Most collectors focus their search on older metal and vinyl kits, released prior to the last steel lunchbox, Rambo, in the early 1980s. Among the most coveted lunch boxes are the dome style boxes, which held the thermos above the meal inside the curved top. Vinyl kits are also considered primo collectibles since they were more easily damaged and destroyed than their steel counterparts.

Values on rectangular metal boxes are determined by age, condition, scene depicted and rarity. Certainly, the boxes from the 1950s and earlier are the highest valued, generally speaking, although certain TV shows and characters boost box values from the 1960s and 70s into triple digits. Boxes with a science fiction or western theme are always in high demand, as are kits featuring other toy collectibles, such as Barbie and Hot Wheels.

Thermoses, too, have attained a collectible status. Often seen individually, they are sought by collectors to complete a kit, or in the hopes of one day finding the matching box. Many sell for $50 or more, without the box!

Pet Rock from Rock Bottom Productions. 1975. $10-15.

Mini-Kiddles pop-up gingerbread house
with doll. 1967 by Mattel. $25-30.

Liddle Kiddles 3 story house.
1968 by Mattel. $20-30.

Dorothy Hammil doll by Ideal. 1975. 12". $45-55.

Uniroyal "Nauga animal". 1960s. $65-75.

1936 Ford classic Hot Wheels car on card. 1967. $50-60.

Peeping Bomb hot wheel with button. (Orange). 1970. $10-15.

Snake Hot Wheels car, with parachute. (yellow stripe). 1970. $85-95.

Mighty Maverick Hot Wheels car, with button. 1970. (green fin). $35-45.

Chaparral Hot Wheels car, with button. ZG-1969. (White fin). $20-25.

Ice "T", Hot Wheels, 1971.(Tall Yella). $40-50.

Santa Fe and Albuquerque reel by View-master with booklet. 1970. $12-15.

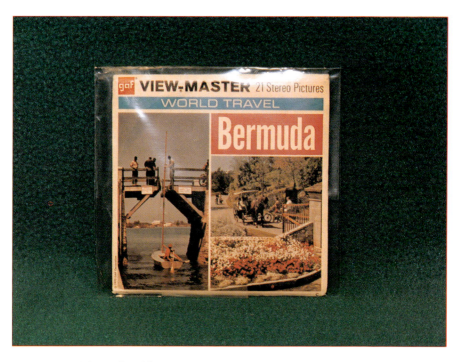

Bermuda world travel reel by View-master with booklet. 1970. $12-15.

Daniel Boone stereo picture for View-master, from the 1960s T.V. show starring Fess Parker. Includes booklet. 1965. $18-25.

Mission Impossible stereo pictures from Mission Impossible. 1968 by View-master. $15-20.

Frankenstein plastic model kit by
Aurora. 1961. $150-175.

Buck Rogers Marauder model by
Monogram. 1979. $20-30.

Explorer 18 satellite model kit by Hawk.
1968. $30-35.

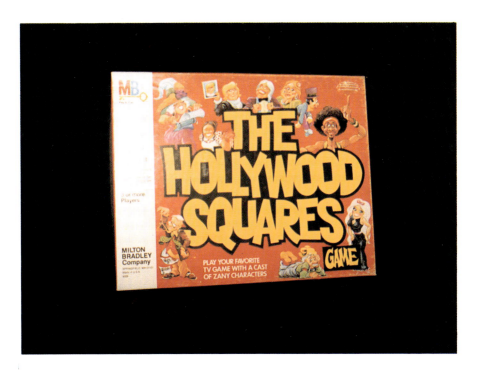

The Hollywood Squares game by Milton Bradley. $10-15.

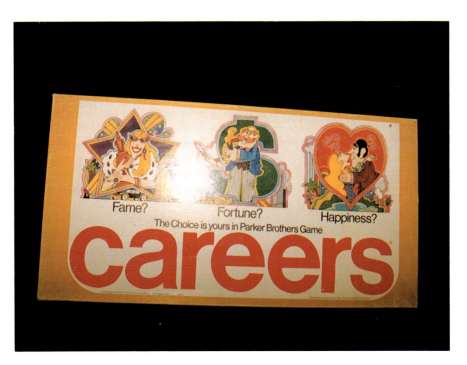

Careers game by Parker Brothers. 1976. $10-15.

The Legend of Jesse James game from Milton Bradley. $80-100.

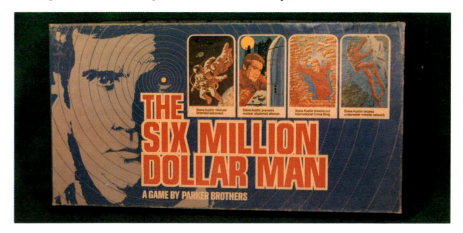

The Six Million Dollar Man game by Parker Brothers. 1975. $10-15.

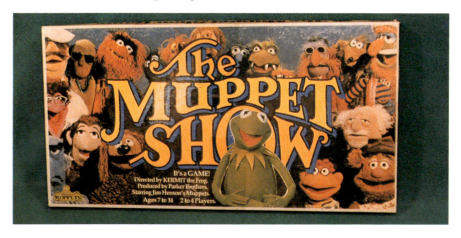

The Muppet Show game by Parker Brothers. 1977. $15-20.

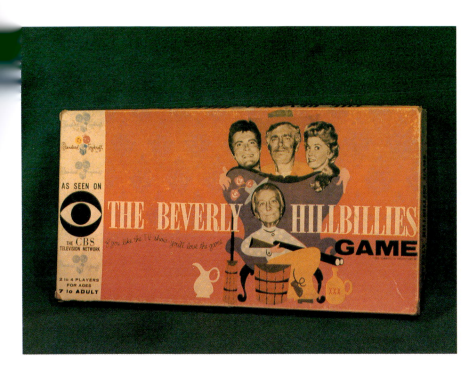

The Beverly Hillbillies game by Standard Toycraft. 1963. $35-45.

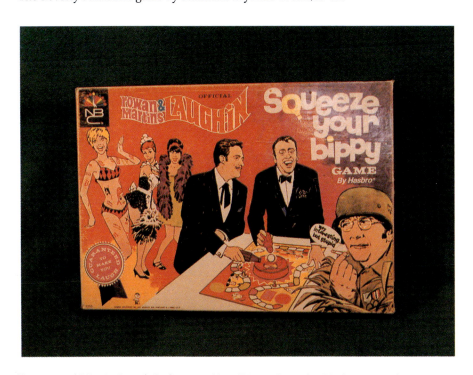

Rowan and Martin Laugh-In Squeeze Your Bippy Game by Hasbro. 1968. $75-85.

Fun Flowers Thingmaker toy by Mattel. 1966. $40-50.

Creeple Peeple Thingmaker toy by Mattel. 1965. $40-50.

The Beverly Hillbillies metal lunch box by Aladdin. $100-125.

The Rat Patrol metal lunch box by Aladdin. 1967. $60-75.

The Banana Splits plastic lunch box with thermos by King Seeley. 1969. $400-450.

Emergency! metal lunch box with thermos by Aladdin. 1973. $65-75.

Pink gingham metal lunch box with thermos by King Seeley. 1976. $40-50.

Barbie and Midge vinyl lunch box with Thermos. 1965. $120-140.

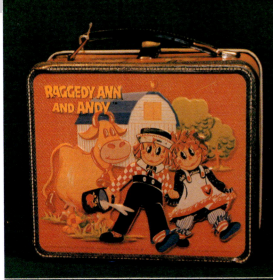

Raggedy Ann and Andy
metal lunch box by
Aladdin. 1973. $20-30.

Wagon Train metal
lunch box with thermos
by King Seeley. 1964.
$65-75.

Star Wars metal lunch box with thermos by King Seeley. 1977. $50-60

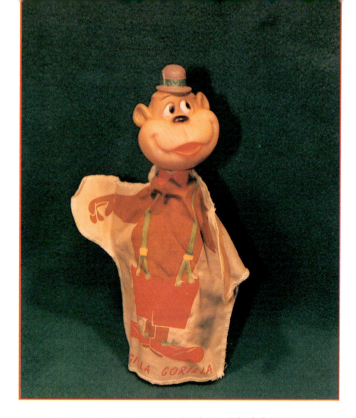

Magilla Gorilla puppet. Mid-60s. Ideal. $45-55.

Stuffed cotton smiling face puppy toy. 1960s. $ 8-12.

MUSIC COLLECTIBLES

ELVIS & THE BEATLES

Music collectibles from the 1950s, 60s and 70s feature a few major players and a host of minor ones. Elvis and the Beatles, of course, lead the pack. The amount of Elvis and Beatles memorabilia staggers even the most determined collectors and the prices for the premium items have rocketed out of sight. Nonetheless, there are lots and lots of people who collect Elvis and Beatles memorabilia, and rest assured that any pre-death Elvis items and any original 60s Beatles items are good investment ideas. Be aware, however, that many of these items have been reproduced, and are, occasionally, falsely represented as original issue.

Oddly, most of the old vinyl records are not really that collectible (with a few major exceptions). There were too many of them. Most of them are not in mint condition, and the entire vinyl market has taken a dive since the advent of CDs. What collectors are primarily after are things like toys, old buttons, dolls, teen accessories, magazine covers, concert tickets, etc.

...AND OTHER TEEN IDOLS

Inspired by the Beatles, a group of clever TV executives crafted and marketed a band called The Monkees in the late 1960s, and today Davy, Micky, Peter and Mike are extremely collectible. A line of comic books, endless teen magazines (including the popular *Monkee Spectaculars*) and a few different versions of the Monkeemobile are among the more popular collectibles, along with more than one set of trading cards and the elusive vinyl Monkees lunchbox.

Similar in audience appeal, The Partridge Family made its debut in the early 1970s, featuring the absolutely dreamy David Cassidy as lead singer Keith Partridge. It was a big hit, resulting in not only great ratings, but also hit songs, several LPs, a lunch box, a board game and several magazine covers (including *TV Guide* and *Life*). Great collectibles.

Bobby Sherman also got his own lunchbox, as did Donny and Marie Osmond. Donny and Marie collectors, in fact, have lots of great stuff to look for, including a complete soundstage playset ($250) and the Donny and Marie dolls, which have some of the best, gaudiest wardrobes in all of doll-dom!

Mego also released a great Cher doll and wardrobe line in the 1970s, along with a Sonny and Cher soundstage playset.

KISS AND OTHER ROCKERS

If your tastes run more toward heavy metal and less toward sugary pop, you are not alone. One of the most collectible of all bands today is KISS, perhaps the zenith of the platformed, made-up, glittery, dry ice, fire-breathing, stage explosions, blood-spiting rock genre. Their albums often contained inserts (a cardboard gun in Love Gun, a decal in Rock & Roll Over), which makes them very collectible in complete and original form. Beyond the albums, there were KISS dolls (highly prized and very valuable), a lunch box, gum cards, belt buckles, comic books, magazines, a licensed toy guitar and more. Basically, anything from the days when they still wore their make-up is considered cool. The KISS fan club, founded in the 1970s, is called the KISS Army. Enough said.

Most rock bands, however, haven't really spawned a wealth of collectibles beyond the realm of albums, 45s and 8-tracks (one day they'll hit, you'll see). The Who and The Rolling Stones at least have some movie memorabilia and for some bands there may be a book or two, perhaps a display item from a music store, a few t-shirts and a Rolling Stone cover. But most rock bands didn't issue a lot of memorabilia that is available to today's collectors.

CONCERT POSTERS & PSYCHEDELIA

During the 1960s and early 1970s, the Fillmore concert hall became noted for its fantastic psychedelic promotional posters. Today, these posters are quite valuable, although some reproductions have been manufactured. Even the reproductions are fast sellers.

These posters are among the most valuable items in the growing field of psychedelia collecting. Lava lamps, Peter Max tennis shoes, love beads, black light posters, op art designs, underground comics and vintage pot-smoking accessories (decorative bongs, hookahs and pipes) are also becoming quite popular. Movie posters such as The Trip and Easy Rider also fall into this category. Watch for this field to mushroom, if you'll excuse the pun.

Opposite page photo:

Ringo Starr doll by Remco. 1964. 5". $95-110.

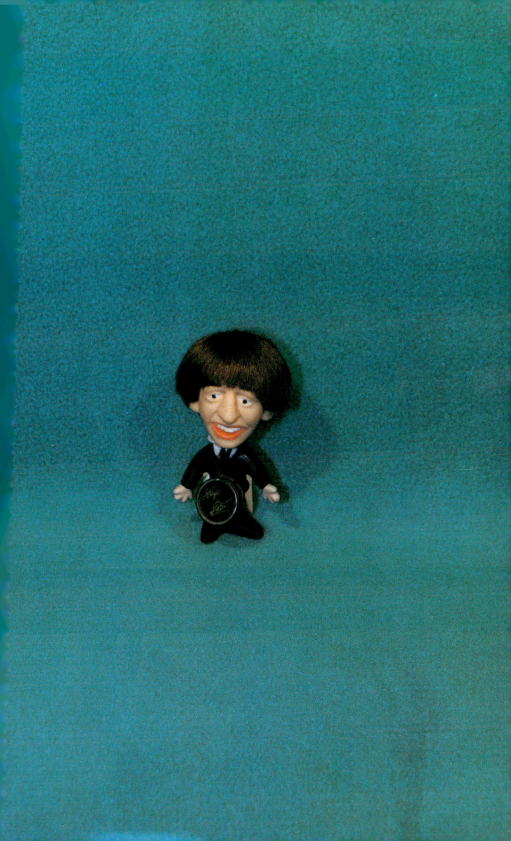

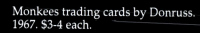

Monkees trading cards by Donruss. 1967. $3-4 each.

Beatles trading cards by Topps. 1960s.
$2-3 each.

Trading cards from Kiss by Donruss.
1978, $1-1.50 each.

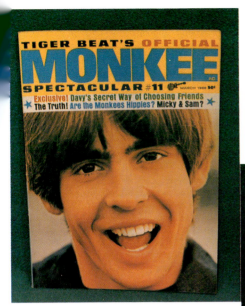

Monkee Spectacular magazine #11. March, 1968. $25- 30.

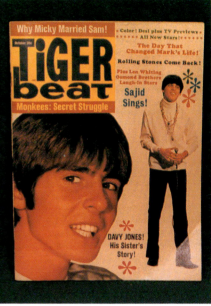

Tiger Beat teen magazine. October, 1968. $15-20.

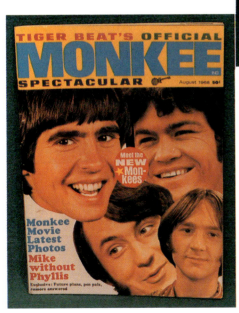

Monkee Spectacular magazine #16. August, 1968. $25-30.

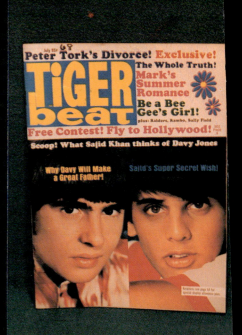

Top left:
Song Hits Magazine. 1972. $10-15.

Top right:
Tiger Beat teen magazine. July, 1968.
$15-20.

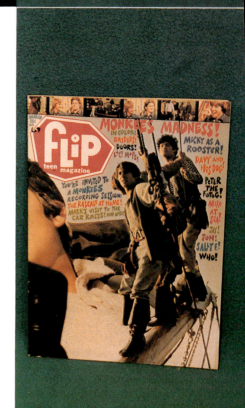

Bottom right:
Flip magazine. March, 1968. $18-20.

Top left:
Song Hits 1972-73 Yearbook. $15-20.

Top right:
Song Hits Magazine. 1975. $15-18.

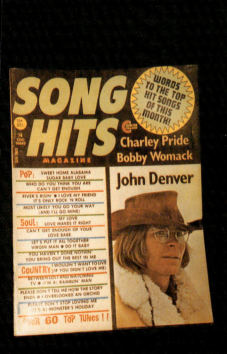

Bottom left:
Song Hits Magazine. 1974. $12-15.

MONKEES 200 WILDEST NEW PIX

OCT/25¢

16
MAGAZINE

MICKY · MARK
"VISIT OUR NEW HOMES"

MONKEES FAB
NEW CLOTHES YOU CAN WIN 'EM EZ

DAVY
COME TO HIS
SURPRISE
PARTY!

BEATLES RING YOUR DING

10 SUPER GLAM
COLOR PIN-UPS
TORK · MARK
RAIDERS · RASCALS
LEWIS & CLARKE & MORE!

MISS 16 CONTEST

KEITH & KEVIN
TRUE FAX & PIX

DD&B
ZZTAP YOU!

FREDDY JOE Jr.
CHARLIE "OUR"
LIVES IN PIX

MONKEES & RAIDERS Take On Madame Merkin! 25¢
MARCH

DIG

Hey, Mark! What's this I hear about 500,000 DIG phone calls?

Don't rub it in, Paul! The whole fantastic STAR NIGHT story's inside!

SALLY FIELDS · FANG Returns!
DOORS · **MONKEES**

Len Whiting's Love Message
How to be Sajid's Best Girl

Mark's New Religion

★★★★★

An Exciting New Fave!
Jimmy Cavaretta

FaVE!
September 36
the newest and the truest!

Special Section: Tiny Tim

All the Facts!

The Strange
Disappearance of
DAVY JONES!
Now Playing: The Monkees' Movie
Plus Raiders, D.D.B, Cowsills

102 MAGIC **MONKEES** PIN-UPS
35 CENTS
DECEMBER 1967
A FAB ALOO

Hullabaloo

DYNAMITE
ERIC BURDON
CONTEST 500 PRIZES
WIN:
PROFESSIONAL
DRUM SET
MIKES
FAB LPs COLOR
POSTERS MORE!

INSIDE SCOOPS
BEE GEES
RASCALS
JEFFERSON
AIRPLANE
BEATLES

PLUS: EXCLUSIVE PICS
PRIVATE LIVES

BIG BOBBY · **SHERMAN SECTION!** ALL YOUR QUESTIONS ANSWERED!

FaVE!
the newest and the truest!

FREE CONTEST: FLY TO HOLLYWOOD!
PREVIEW: SAJID'S SPECIAL! · Are the
MONKEES Afraid to Replace
PETER? · FRID'S NEW GROUP! · CHRIS
JONES' WILD LOVE! · Are You the
Girl for LEN WHITING?

Opposite page photos:

Top left:
16 Magazine. October, 1967. $4-6.

Top right:
Dig magazine. March, 1968. $15-20.

Bottom left:
Hullabaloo magazine. December, 1967. $20-25.

Bottom right:
Fave magazine. June, 1969. $20-25.

Center:
Fave magazine. September, 1968. $20-25.

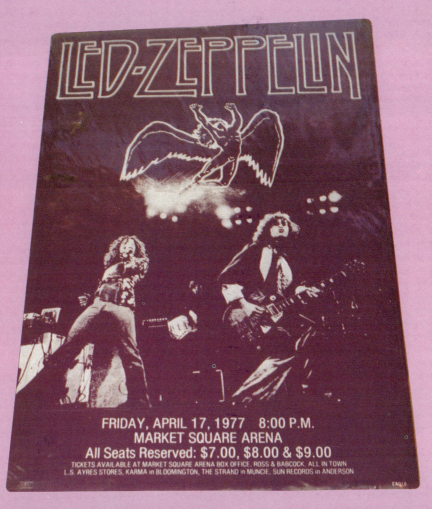

Led-Zeppelin poster. 1977. 13" x 20". $65-75.

FUNKY TEXTILES, GROOVY THREADS & PLATFORM SHOES

The vintage clothing market is huge in the 1990s, and many of the most sought-after styles originated in the 1950s, 60s and 70s.

In the 1950s, fabric patterns enjoyed a heyday. Wild, adventurous prints, bold colors and super-modern geometric shapes were fashionable and popular. At the same time, decorators were lured by the Donna Reed syndrome, so many textiles looked sweet, homey and just plain cute.

In the kitchen, especially, tea towels, aprons and curtains were sunny, bright, often whimsical and always darling. Today, these styles are sought by collectors and fans of the June Cleaver school of kitchen design. We give them an "A."

WOMEN'S FASHIONS

The good news is that there was lots of variety in women's fashions during the 1950s, 60s and 70s. By the mid-1970s, women could choose from mini-, midi- or maxi-lengths. Glitter and Gunne Sax were both considered stylish. Freedom of expression was encouraged. Today, the styles that have garnered the most attention are some of the most extreme.

Poodle skirts, bobby socks and saddle oxfords have survived since the 1950s as a stylish statement. Also popular from that decade: gaudy chiffon prom dresses!

Brightly-colored mini-dresses and clothes made out of shiny vinyl are considered very chic among the retro crowd. Accent the look with fishnet hose and a pair of shiny white crinkle-vinyl knee-high boots for best results!

What's not collectible in vintage clothing? Pants suits, bad polyester and tube tops. Maybe in a few years...

SHOES, HATS, HANDBAGS AND ACCESSORIES

Trying to find vintage platform shoes, GoGo Boots or Beatle Boots today is like searching for the Holy Grail. Everyone wants them, and no one seems to have them. Vintage clothing stores seem to suck the great shoes out of thrift stores before they even hit the shelves, and even if you manage to find a pair you like in a vintage clothing store, what are the odds that they'll fit you? It can be a frustrating quest, but if you manage to find that perfect pair of silver glitter platforms, it all seems worth the effort. A great pair of shoes can make or break a vintage outfit.

Hats, too, can offer the perfect finishing touch to a really retro look. A fake leopard skin pillbox hat is one of the ultimate fashion statements of the early 60s. Jackie Kennedy popularized the look of the pillbox hat, and today, the Jackie look remains popular among certain sects of the young urban chic.

A slew of purse styles were popular in the 50s, 60s and 70s and are considered collectible today. Clear plastic purses with flowers or small items visibly trapped inside are very hot. Remember wooden purses that were decoupaged and varnished? Still cool. How about bright shiny patent leather shoulder bags with huge buckles. Yes. Some of today's most cutting edge fashionites are opting to carry vintage lunch boxes as handbags, a great idea!

During the 1950s, rhinestone jewelry enjoyed a golden age. Today, many pieces are very collectible, including big bracelets, broaches, necklaces and rings. For a more mod look, try an original plastic GoGo ring, a Rat Fink ring, a 1970s mood ring, or a POW bracelet! Around your neck - a lavender velvet choker is perfect.

MEN'S WEAR

What girl can resist a guy in jeans, a white t-shirt and a leather jacket? The classic 1950s biker look is still a popular favorite today.

Bellbottoms and big pointy collars have also re-emerged in a big way in certain circles. Medallions go nicely with that look. Neru collars, although hard to find, look good today, as does the classic Man from U.N.C.L.E. black turtleneck look.

Hawaiian shirts are a safe bet for a great retro look, as is summery 60s surf bum attire.

Fat ties and leisure suits, however, have not yet become cool.

Yellow cotton apron with rickrack trim. 1950s. $5-8.

Red cotton apron with cross stitched trim. 1950s. $8-10.

Pink organza apron. 1960s. $6-9.

Green checkered cotton apron. 1950s. $5-8.

Red polka dot collar and hat. 1950s. $15-20 set.

Cotton floral tea towel. 1950s. $5-7.

Cotton tea towel with strawberries. 1950s. $4-6.

Linen tea towel with embroidered china plate. 1960s. $7-10.

Linen tea towel with embroidered pots and pans. 1960s. $7-10.

Leather strap high heel shoes. 1960s. $15-20.

Plastic gold color lady's shoes with brass buckles. 70s. $5-8.

Mesh lady's shoes with leather back trim. 1970s. $6-10.

Leather lady's shoes with black buttons. 1960s. $15-20.

Wooden purse from Enid Purse Co. 1970s. $20-25.

Wooden purse from Enid Box Co. 1970s. $35-45.

Wooden purse from Enid Box co. 1970s. $30-40.

Jeweled handbag with burlap and leather trim. 1960s. $25-35.

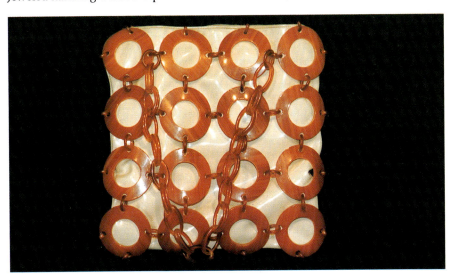

Purse with plastic rings and plastic insert by Paco Rebanna. 1960s. $40-50.

Plastic handbag with lace trim inserted.
1950s. $5-8.

Plastic lipstick mirror and cover in
original case. 1950s. $4-6.

Jeweled handbag with burlap and leather trim. 1960s. $30-35.

Striped silk umbrella with wooden handle. 1950s. $8-12.

Silk umbrella with plastic handle. 1960s. $5-8.

PAPER POWER

MEGABUCKS FOR MAGAZINES

A number of magazines published in the 1950s, 60s and 70s have gathered huge collector followings over the years. Among the most collected titles: *Playboy, Famous Monsters of Filmland, Rolling Stone, MAD, TV Guide* and *Life*. Many collectors choose to narrow the search by category, for instance collecting only space-related Life magazines, or just the *TV Guides* with Lucille Ball on the cover.

The first issue of *Playboy*, featuring Marilyn Monroe, was published in December 1953, and is today valued at up to $2,000. Few other magazines from any decade can touch that one. The first *TV Guide*, with Lucy, Desi and their new baby on the cover (April 1953), sells for $300, while the first issue of *Famous Monsters*, published in 1958, sells for $400. MAD #1 (October 1952), in comic book format, brings about $2,000-2,500 in good condition.

COMIC BOOKS: SOARING TO SUPER PRICES

Today, most people are aware that comic books are valuable collectibles. In the 1950s, 60s and 70s, however, people just didn't think of them that way. That is why it is so wonderful to find an old comic book that has been kept in good condition, and that is why many of them have become so valuable.

The most collectible arena in comic books is, by far, the superhero format. And, during the 1950s, 60s and 70s, some wonderful comics were published, which, today, command top dollar.

Early issues of *Batman, Superman, Spiderman, The Fantastic Four* and *X-Men* are especially collectible. So are comics featuring character origins stories, death of a character, important costume changes and the introduction of a major character. *Fantastic Four* #48 (March 1966), which introduces the Silver Surfer, for instance, is valued at about $500-600.

Other comic book styles, such as "funny animals," Archies, westerns and most TV and movie-related comics are also collectible, although their audience is much smaller. Archie comics, romance comics and most cartoon-character comics have not seen the price escalation the superhero comics have enjoyed, perhaps because most of today's comic collectors are young or middle-aged men.

One of the most collected types of comic books, outside of the superhero format, is the underground comic. Original printings of *Mr. Natural, The Fabulous Furry Freak Brothers* and a host of other titles are very collectible to the right audience. Undergrounds were especially popular in the 1970s, and usually included stories about drugs and sex.

HOW TO JUDGE A BOOK

Collectible books from the 1950s, 60s and 70s cover a wide range of interests. Sleazy exploitation paperbacks with titles like "Blonde and Deadly" are collected as are slightly more respectable mystery paperbacks with lurid content and great covers.

Also, certain authors boost book prices, including Philip K. Dick, Fredric Brown, Raymond Chandler and Jack Kerouac.

Many people choose to collect older children's books. Public school-issued primary readers featuring Dick and Jane can bring $30-$60 each. Series books, such as The Hardy Boys, Nancy Drew and Tom Swift have inspired many a collector, as have the Whitman authorized TV novelizations, released in hard cover between the late 1950s and the mid-1970s.

Whitman also published a line of Big Little Books, which are very collectible today, both in hard- and later soft-cover editions.

Perhaps one of the most successful collectible book lines issued in the 1950s, 60s and 70s is the Little Golden Books line from Western Publishing. Baby Boomers can't resist these little, easy-to read souvenirs of childhood, and most collectors are especially looking for titles they remember as kids. Vintage Little Golden Books typically sell for $5-20, and first editions can be identified by an "A" appearing in the lower right corner of the back page.

WHEN TRADING CARDS CAME WITH GUM

Trading cards, both sports and non-sports, have existed for decades, and are extremely popular collectibles today. Cards from the 50s, 60s and 70s, typically issued with chewing gum in a "wax pack," can command surprising prices. Card collectors care about condition, and try to find cards with sharp corners, good printing registration, an even cut, no fading or folding. Never use a rubber band to hold a set of cards together.

The sports card hobby exploded in the early 1990s and has since calmed somewhat. Those collectors primarily seek older 1950s cards and cards depicting specific players, especially Rookie cards from the player's first year as a professional ball player. Football cards, though less prevalent than baseball cards, are highly collectible, too.

One very collectible card is a Mickey Mantle card issued in an April 1963 issue of *Life* magazine, featuring Liz and Dick in Cleopatra garb on the cover. An interior cereal ad was accompanied by two baseball cards, stitched into the magazine. If found intact, the magazine sells for about $200.

Outside the sports arena, trading cards relating to TV, movies, comics and music are always popular. Among the best bets are Outer Limits, original Star Trek cards, KISS, Tarzan and Superman cards. Beatles cards are fairly common today, and sell for about $2 each (B&W or color). The Gilligan's Island set, on the other hand, is among the most difficult to complete.

One of the most collectible sets of the early 1960s was called Mars Attacks and featured some great, gory scenes of Martians killing people, pets and more. This set was reprinted in the early 1990s and again in 1995, and was also imitated in a newer series called Dinosaurs Attack.

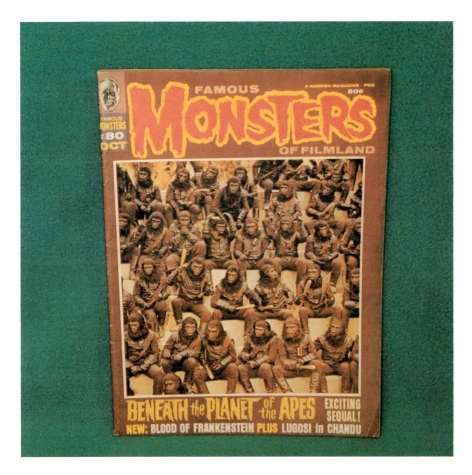

Famous Monsters of Filmland magazine #80, October, 1970. $10-15.

Famous Monsters of Filmland magazine #50, July, 1968. $20-30.

Famous Monsters magazine #155, July,1979. $8-12.

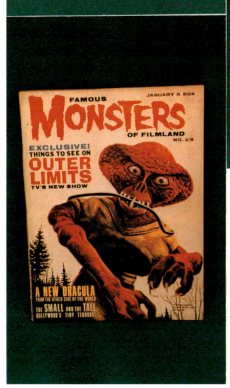

Famous Monsters of Filmland magazine #26, January, 1964. $70-80.

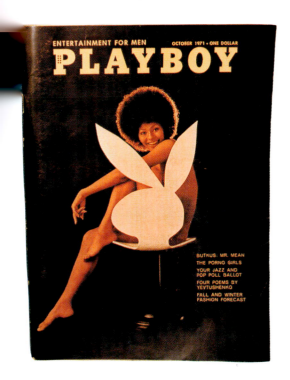

Playboy magazine. October, 1971. $9-12.

Playboy magazine with Raquel Welsh on the cover. December, 1979. $15-22.

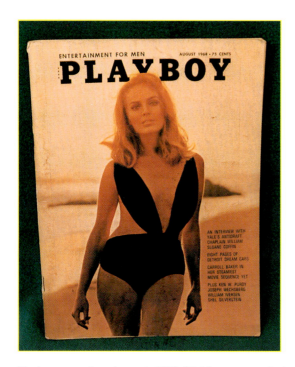

Playboy magazine. August, 1968. $8-10.

Playboy magazine. October, 1969. $6-8.

Playboy magazine. March, 1962. $15-20.

Playboy magazine. June, 1965. $15-20.

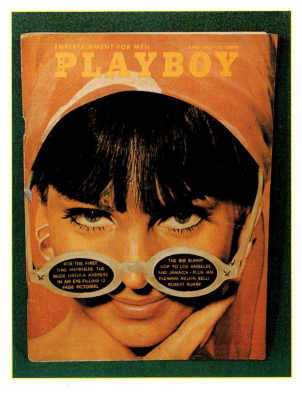

Top left:
Hee Haw magazine. 1971. $12-15.

Top right:
Hee Haw Gags and Gals, Songs and Fun.
1974. $6-8.

Bottom right:
Hee Haw magazine. 1971. $12-15.

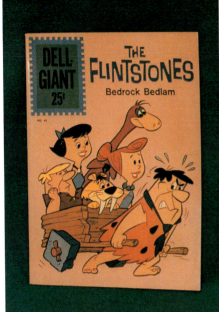

Flintstone #1 comic by Dell Giant
Comics. 1961. $185-210.

Jonny Quest #1 by Gold Key Comics.
1964. $50-60.

Snooper and Blabber #1 by Gold Key
Comics. 1962. $45-55.

Mr. and Mrs. J. Evil Scientists by Gold
Key Comics. 1963. $18-25.

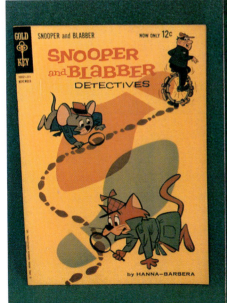

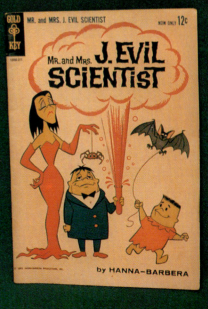

Top left:
Peter Parker Spectacular Spider-Man #1 by
Marvel Comics. 1976. $40-45.

Top right:
The Incredible Hulk 4#181 by Marvel
Comics. 1974. $250-275.

Bottom right:
The Fantastic Four #12 by Marvel
Comics. 1962. $75-85.

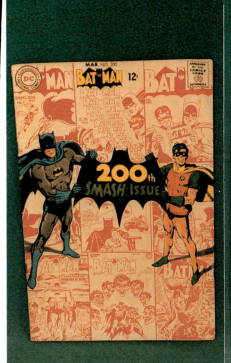

Top left:
Batman 200th Smash Issue by D.C.
Comics. 1968. $30-35.

Top right:
Swamp Thing #1 by D.C. Comics. 1972.
$50-60.

Bottom left:
Justice League of America #21 by D.C.
Comics. 1963. $45-55.

Top left:
Kamandi #1 by D.C. Comics. 1972. $30-35.

Bottom left:
Underground adult *Funny Aminals* #1 by Apex Novelties. 1972. $25-30.

Bottom right:
Underground adult *Air Pirate Funnies* by Hell Comics. 1971. Disney sued and this was immediately pulled. $50-60.

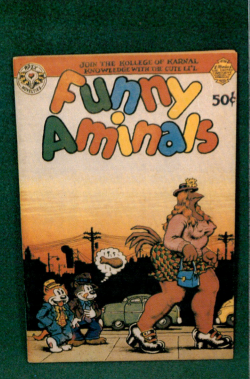

op right:
The Lucy Show #1 by Gold Key Comics.
1963. $55-65.

Bottom left:
My Favorite Martian #1 by Gold Key.
1963. $30-40.

Bottom right:
Starforce magazine. July, 1978. $5-8.

Foul by Connie Hawkins. $5-8.

Pro Football 1966 by Jack Zanger. $8-12.

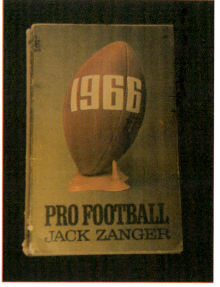

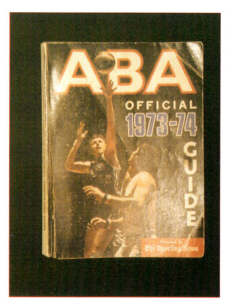

ABA Official 1973-74 Guide. $10-15.

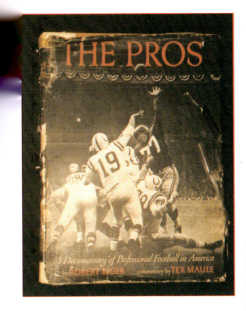

The Pros by Robert Riger. 1960. $8-12.

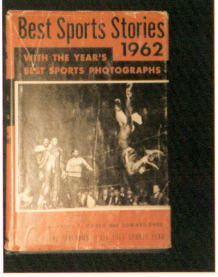

Best Sports Stories 1962, a photographic study by Marsh and Dutton. $15-20.

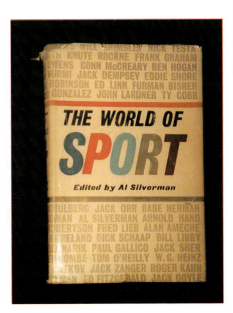

The World of Sport by Al Silverman. 1962. $7-10.

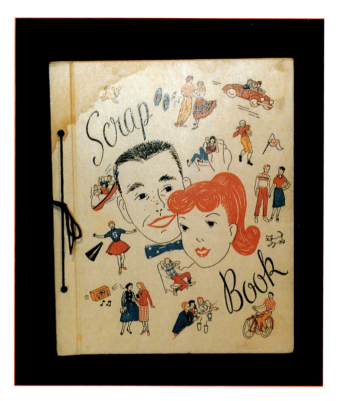

Scrap book. 1950s. $7-10.   *The Jetsons* "Golden book". 1962. $15-20.

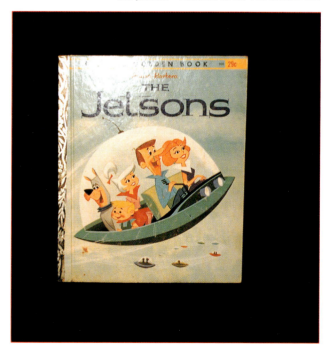

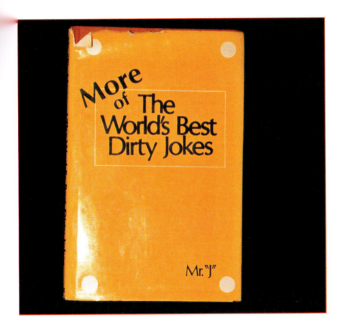

More of the World's Best Dirty Jokes by Mr. "J". Citadel press, 1970. $6-10.

Jonathan Livingston Seagull game by Mattel. 1960. $12-15.

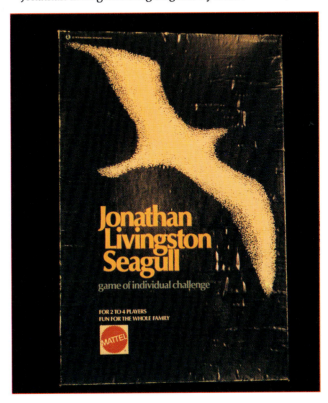

Odd Rods trading cards by Donruss.
1970s. $2-3 each.

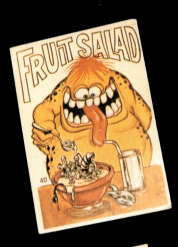